POETIC UNIVERSALISMS

Volume II

LENA SMITH CARTER

POETIC UNIVERSALISMS

VOLUME II

Copyright © 2006 by Lena Smith Carter as a compilation of original poetry.

The poems in this work are an original collection of poetry submitted to the manufacturer by the named individual author/publisher. The author /publisher confirms the authenticity of the poetry and the manufacturer is neither liable nor obligated to authenticate.

The views expressed in this book do not reflect the views of the manufacturer or members of the manufacturing staff. These views are solely inured to the author/publisher.

Under the copyright laws of the United States of America, this book is protected, with all the rights and privileges appertaining thereto. This book may not be reproduced, shared, electronically reproduced, nor copied by any other means not approved by written consent of the author.

Manufactured in the United States of America

by

www.lulu.com

ISBN: 978-0-6151-3654-7

DEDICATION

To my children:

Ehrika Aileen Carter Gladden
Jessica Faye Carter
David George Carter, Jr.
Blayne Anthony Gladden
Jennifer Mary Gallagher Carter

You continue to make me proud of you with all your sharing, caring, loving, giving, and hard work. I am grateful to God for your successes and know that the future holds only good for all of you. As you know, I do not believe there is anything we do that is more important than working hard to turn out productive citizens for our society. I believe that was done and I am eternally grateful to have been chosen by you.

FOREWORD

In our nation, there are many injustices which occur everyday. We seem to be overrun by violence, murder, war, broken relationships, failures, deceptive politicians, failing schools, et.al. However, one thing is certain: We still have peace here on the homefront, although we have had a few blemishes. The children still play, they still sing songs, and aren't we lucky as a nation to be able to sit with them in the park; have the opportunity to consider such brilliant pastimes as concerts, ballets, operas, sporting events, vacations, art shows, movies, creative writing, and poetry.

We can fully participate or simply participate as a spectator, for "when the tree falls in the forest, if you didn't hear it, did it still fall?" If your son or daughter writes a beautiful, passage, will that talent be magnified or stifled? *You* have the power to encourage or crush their ambition. Do not always take what you see at face value. Remember the greatest poets of all time often had hidden meanings that could only resonate when experience allowed your understanding of the words and deeply felt emotions.

When we start to complain, we should remember that many people die every day for the freedoms that we enjoy and that every day spent making life better for others especially through creative writing, music, dance, poetry, shows, operas, ballets, etc., is a treasure that we are afforded; we should nurture those tendencies in our children.

This book of poetry explores life's journey in double and single-word titles and if you have lived any of life, you will see yourself in these pages.
Subsequent volumes will explore a volume of two-word titles mixed with one-word titles from the previous publication, two-word titles, three-word titles, and other mixtures, increasing the number of words in subsequent titles. There will be ten-twenty volumes and hopefully they will remind you of some of your life's happiest times!

                            Lena Smith Carter
                        dseyafanel@hotmail.com

SHATTERED DREAMS

Stoically I sit and consider wishes made,
Framed pictures make their way only to invade
my troubled mind,
I look, I see, I remember all;
Especially the events which eventually swayed.

I knew the things I wanted,
I pursued a path unclear,
And beat my way, though often mired,
In difficulties and fear.

Life gave times too tough to weather,
And cried, I often did,
But then persisted in my pursuits.
Inner thoughts? I hid!

I aimed in a direction
And thoroughly followed my plan,
Yet matters converged and wrecked attempts,
Providing a persistent ban!

Months came and years passed by,
Small steps were made and cheered,
I tried, I failed, and yet I held,
My dreams contained; to me endeared.

PEACE

Doves and olive branches,
Signs of every kind,
Appear so man can n'er forget
"It is the tie that binds."

Children play and sing their songs,
While we wait in the park,
The blessedness of that event
Will really make its mark.

To concerts we will go,
To ballets we'll appear,
All games to view; the skies are clear,
Security is near.

The streams run clear, the clouds appear,
We whisper in the wind,

No nuclear blight, no shadowy sights,
Mutual concord's 'round the bend.

LIMITED REGRETS

One desires a lovely fountain,
Within view and overflowing,
Cobblestones and ice blue seas
Joy in the soul, glowing!

So many things went by
And I in no way worried
That what I did not see
Would disappear unless I hurried.

There were times I could have gone
And could not bring myself to travel,
I had to spend a day or two
Decidedly configuring babble.

If only . . .

PROVOCATION

Stroll along the avenue,
Moist with morning's dew,
Wear your finest garb
Contacts here are few.

From a distant window,
Lips as red as flame,
She watches and she waits alone,
Perched and tame!

She'll bide her time while watching
Your every maneuvering tension,
Mordacious in her style, yet
Intenerate in her invention!

CORNERING ENERGY

Distant runs around the park,
Never ending trails,
Sparkling water close beside,
Forming streams as squirrels prevail!

Lift the branches above my head,
Water's near the end,
Dodge the weeds, stay off the grass,
Exhaustion 'round the bend!

Fall upon the grass,
Raise your left leg high,
Move the leaves, turn your head,
Relinquish a cumbrous sigh.

Strain your body to its lengths,
Stretch each sinewy mainstay,

Slowly through manipulation,
    Elasticity day to day!

NEGLECT

Left alone to contemplate,
Bygone days and stellar times,
Picturesque scenes come across my mind
As mellow words appear and rhyme.

Gently taking into question
With the new day what I'll see,
Take a long walk, look and listen,
Kick the rocks and rub a tree!

Leaving this secluded station,
I recoil and then show fear
Toward the thought of non remembrance,
Towards the things I've held so dear.

INCENDIARY WORDS

Truth is often skirted,
As tales are fiercely wound,
Piercing through the reputation,
Pressing to the ground!

Dreams, desires, and longings,
Held within my soul
Of climbing, scrambling entities,
Within a dimension bold.

Utterances often leave a mark,
      Decurrent
           in
              their
                 direction,
Destructive! Causing derision!
Leaving indications of a need for protection!

PATIENCE

Sitting very quietly
Rocking the wicker chair,
Awaiting your arrival,
Leisurely in my lair.

Branches dipping low,
They tend peacefully to sway,
Cloudy lines across the sky
Melting cares away!

Starlight brightly glittering,
Raindrops falling, splattering!
I'm not anxious in my waiting,
Distant memories calming,

UNFOUNDED WHISPERINGS

Quiescent thought cannot confound,
Deep ramblings from within,
They're passed and scattered to the winds
Of gossip on a whim.

Your high regard will be damaged
As if it never existed,
Derogatory rumors burn the earth!
Umph! Quite twisted!

Unsubstantiated isms passed along
With crude intentions,
Pierce the conscience like needles,
Lending less than honorable mention.

COMPLIANCE

Kneeling down beside the road
I see a pilfered treasure,
Lying just beyond me,
And I stop and think and measure,
What this means, should I take it,
Should I just pass by?

From my mother's sagacious arsenal
Of many saws of do's and don'ts,
I take aim at handling gently
Prizes that will not come back to haunt!

Think well!
Remember all!
Protect integrity!
Act reasonably!

SECLUDED ISLAND

You yawn, you stretch and then you wake
To avian melodies fragmented,
Glints of sunshine, ferns sway gently,
O'er fruits effervescently fermented.

The fog rolls in; the waters splash
To repetitive head high gushes,
You seek a ridge without a cover,
Hmmm! Emotional rushes!!

Garlands, buds, and yellow blades
Reveal a knack for finding
Beauty clothed in vegetation,
Fragrance of frangipani binding!

Petals floating on the breeze,
Wafting gingerly o'er limbs,
Wispy clouds, sun-warmed rocks,
Waning sunlight, dim!

DISOBEDIENCE

Tiptoe past the screen door,
Crawl upon the floor,
It's just a few more inches,
I'll grab it while he snores.

"Who's that out there? Who?"
Comes the interrogation,
I freeze, I sit, I crawl, I slide,
Before the sudden abruption.

Should I return to claim my prize?
I've just begun to ponder,
Peppermint balls and cherry jawbreakers,
All inspire wonder!!

Tiptoe in, make no sound,
Make an extravagant wish,

"Who is that who slithered in and
　　Clinked the candy dish?"

CONTOURED DESIRES

Shapes affect our lives in ways
That do not seem to accumulate;
For often we are unaware
How readily shape can stimulate.

He crossed the street unaware
Of spinal curves observed
Of shoulders square of angled chin,
What womankind deserves!

What caught your fancy as you combed
The world for your great lover,
Fittingly mounds, shapely rounds
Beneath the predator's hover!

UNIVERSALITY

Spanning time and seeming often
Immortal in its teeming,
Enveloping elements abound like the
Sunshine in its beaming!

Art, love, music, prayer,
Greed, color, hate and religion,
All needed as an implement
As if an elaborate contagion!

On the canvas, on your chaise,
In your ears and in your pose,
In your heart and on your skin,
In your mind and in your soul!

Be they visual or elusive,
Or emotional in their presence;
They appear and carry substance
Making entrance to our conscience.

AUTUMNAL HAZE
(Love, Seasons, Life, Wonder!)

Rise slowly from eastward, O western setting sun!
Blaze
Anew! Get up, swell the human spirit says
Your constant companion moon of days,
Lending wonder to cardinals, chickadees and 'jays
Who constantly concertize and amaze
Passersby who are in awe of the glaze
Of glory you send!   The laze
Of summer creeps upon the landscape, pays
A visit with the promise of ways
To leisurely wind our maze
Through vines tightly wound and gaze
Upon seashore, sand, and plum trees which raise
Our thoughts to delightful eating pleasures; a craze
Of oranges, cinnamons, and chocolates; sways
On breezes, lightly dancing across a phase
Of the setting sun; with piercing yeas
I cheer, settling on her face, the autumnal haze

Reflecting in counterpoint to raze
Prior passages and issue nays!
Recreate browns and grays
Metamorphosizing to new clays!

RESTLESSNESS

Time waits for no one,
You chase it day and night,
In dreams you sit and dance and play,
At times you run in fright!

Tension, pressure, passion, pleasure,
All disturb your calm,
Yet reaches for a higher realm
Ignites a new alarm.

Go swiftly now and charge ahead,
Complete the things you must,
Wondering how to stem the tide
From now until you're dust.

PUZZLING THOUGHTS

Do I like the opera or
Concerts in the park,
Ballet scenes and musical shows,
A nice two hours spent!

Flower shows and poetry readings,
Leisure time's a must,
Lunches, dinners, diamond shopping,
Libraries, discussions of trusts!

Dance and piano lessons,
Stops for lemonade,
Mall treks, brownie galas,
Boy scout pick-ups, baseball cards to trade.

"Were you able to get a deal
That we might eat today?"

"Yes! One dollar for five pasta boxes was all I had to pay."

CURIOSITY

We must take the time to stop
And think of questions of the past,
And all new facts that come
Will bring knowledge that will last.

Crystal balls and spider webs
Can sublimate my mind,
And all other prime encounters
Will catalyze in kind!

Billowy clouds, ill-shaped trees,
Thunder and lightning all!
Glaciers in their majesty,
Can icebergs bring the fall?

Awestruck by the myriad mysteries
Which are presently unsolved,

Does the deep desire to know
Cause ingenuities to evolve?

LIKE IMARI

The glass one, milk clear,
Translucent at its edges,
Like teeth that nature bestows
Smooth to their ridges.

The psyche then impacted
By a floral entity,
Driven to arrive on edge and fringe
Yet to it's center central.

Hold it gently, do not falter,
For its fragility is fixate.
Mind the tensions you apply,
Tabletop linens await!

Many stare with focused gazes,
Soaking in its frangible beauty,

Velvet cloths would be insufficient,
To handle this true treasure!

HOSTILITY

Fomenting emotions surface,
Angst is incurred,
Lending conflict-minded notions
To solutions offered, rendered, and discarded.
Opposition sweeps in,
Crosses lanes of incoming denials
With scathing attempts at acceptance
But rejection creeps to the edge!

PRELAPSARIAN LOVE

Leaves are there for tasting,
Water flows to seeming boils,
Frogs and butterflies
Gently light on shoulders, lips ,
and fingertips!

We walk, we prance through waterfalls,
Roaming, wandering chatting,
We twiddle our fingers, twirl our hair,
Drink nectar from honeysuckles and swallow petals!

Reds, blues, and purples!
Oranges and lavender, in their beauty!
Blues, pinks, and yellows. . .as if an omen sounding!
Then comes the patterns of diamondbacks,
Some coral, green, and black.

We eat though we're not hungry,
New stories we believe,
No decision did we need,
Yet, made one. Yes we did!

AND THEN...

POSSESSION

Hide this box and tell your friends
You have a new obsession,
Spread new gossip, renounce confidences,
All without regression.

After they have disappeared
Creep silently away,
Reclaim your box and open it,
Take the time to play!

Rub the smooth, cool borders,
Finger recessed chinks,
Shine the impearled surfaces,
To opalescent pink!

Add a perfumed ball,
The butler's patina rampant,

Retain the treasured keepsake,
Effulgence is apparent!

EVENTUAL CONNECTIONS

Kids at play, teeter-tottering,
Writing in the sand,
Playing baseball, hide and seek,
Games of every kind!

Soon they talk; still chat and play,
But odd long walks and sunset lingerings,
Late arrivals, dinner skipped,
Telephone homework at midnight!

Movies will soon enter the fray,
Dimples deep as puddles,
Popcorn, cookies, hot chocolates,
Add a little late night ride, chips and cake!
Coffee?

Off in different directions,
Our thoughts will often turn
To days and years and times gone by
Catalogued by scents!

I think of you at coffee,
Remembrances of your perfume invades,
You are not here yet popcorn, chips, and cakes
Are all consistent reminders.

My nine-year-old writes in the sand,
I sit and reminisce,
A child with flowing hair appears,
Dimples deep as puddles!

The swing chains clink beside me,
The scent of your perfume invades.
You're here? . . .

REFLECTIONS

Blackberries, dewberries, yellow plums,
Occupied our time,
All our walks on dangerous roads,
Punctuated by limes!

Mirrored lakes and tiny fish,
Needles from the pines,
Sumac berries soured our taste,
Strawberries on the vine!

Arriving home we climbed the trees
And sat on opposite sides,
Cherries, cherries, cherries, Wow!
Playtime coincides!

GOLDEN SHACKLES

Bracelets, earrings, watches all,
Worn with majestic splendor,
Belts, shoe brooches, walking canes
Tipped, shining like cinders!

Filigree in dresses,
Scarf rings widely used,
Rings and preset sapphires,
A real elaborate ruse!

Emeralds the size of apples,
Pearls of every size and shape,
Diamonds on the bra,
Shining through transparency, from afar!

Leaving here for Washington!
"No, cannot be done.

No security can cover this".
Elaborately chained!!

MEMENTO

Islands, palm trees, caves, and fog,
Lend a calm retreat,
As I gather drink and handfans,
Mindful of the heat!

Retracing all our deliberate steps,
Time could not erase,
The day we made the auspicious walk
To this memorable place!

Hidden by the oxblood foliage,
Translucent, and quite low,
Carved upon the tree trunk words,
Left here long ago!

SILK SCARF

Tumbling, mounding
Slithering on my shoulder; seams unfelt.
Wind the shredded corners,
Tuck them delicately into my belt.

Lift the corner in triangular fashion,
Filch the corner from the brooch,
String the flimsy corners over
To
      c
       a
        s
         c
          a
           d
            e
during my approach!
Colors streaming, wrinkles easing
Their presence seems to mark the threads,

The filature, one by one, extracted
From the cocoon beds!!

ILLUMINATED ORB

Do you think it's there? Who knows!
There is skepticism of things scientific in their origin;
Moon and stars so far away!
How can I tell the source of their light?

The sun is bright and warms the earth,
And then the moon appears
The stars are bright with every turn;
Constellations rage!

Earth is seen from far above,
At night, it gives appearances of light.
Inner core or artificial?
Waiting for the sun?

Is light tangible?
Illuminate at will?

Does moon have light or does it wait
For touches from the sun?

SATISFACTION

Settled here within these walls,
Vases overrun,
Mahogany, cedar, silk brocades,
Ambrosia freshly done!

Music raises harmonious hope,
The oven brings repast,
Nuts and whipped cream mixed together
Satisfies at last!

Day is done, the night has come,
Don the floor length gown,
Mired in the flannel sheets,
Comforted by the down!

It's day, I'm here, the night is gone,
Impressions to arouse,

Rays of sunshine tempt the panes,
    Peeping from the clouds!

SHRINKING LILIES

Stately in their presence,
Blades shimmer lightly,
Buds are set to spring forth,
Colors blazing on!

Through wind and rain and insect attacks,
They're kissed again by warmth,
They rise, they wave, and stand again,
To face another day!

September coolings, October chills,
And then November's bite,
Materializes and attacks
The caudad of their season!

Beaten from yellow to ecru,
And then to straw-like tan,

Their beauty still lies deep within,
 Awaiting spring tide's scan!

DESTINY

Many sets of circumstances
Cross our paths and then,
Lull us on our journey,
'til the bitter end.

No one knows where he goes
Or from whence he came,
Predetermined happenings
Keep him in the game.

Fortune comes to some of us
And others stay dirt poor,
But irresistible powers come
Almost directing a tour!

TORRENTIAL EMOTIONS

The soul stirs at your birth,
You breathe, you cry, you laugh,
Your journey begins and you make memories
Without even knowing when!

Those around you teach you much,
After you're born, you grow, you strive
And deep within, personality develops,
As still you thrive.

Anger, hate, love, envy,
Greed, hostility, all,
You've felt, you've grappled, you've suppressed,
You've hidden much behind a wall.

Through experience you've controlled
And managed many overflows,
The trigger's there to spark, to boil,
To raise to fever pitch!

Personalities differ and often
Some need a little test,
To soften life's blows, control one's mind
And regulate emotional effusiveness.

HOSPITALITY

We were welcomed to the inn,
Remaining somewhat wary,
We didn't know this quiet place
And knew we shouldn't hurry!

We walked through glens, along babbling brooks,
And crossed on stones reclined,
We smelled the honeysuckle blossoms
Hanging from the vine.

With that, relaxed and calm,
We then approached the door,
That opened wide and welcomed us,
Tall urns upon the floor.

Tinkling wind chimes pealed,
Tied on sconces room by room,
The fireplace was stacked with logs,
Without impending doom.

IMPENDING SENECTITUDE

May and June, how light I feel,
Sensations mildly rousing,
Living, loving, laughing, dancing,
All good times espousing!

Children have come and gone,
My spring is long past,
Yet summer leaves a little time
And autumn comes at last!

Evidence of decades comes,
I color with a frenzy,
Some of the now long days are fraught
With aching, throbbing cadenzas!

Slowly December comes,
I watch with vision dim,

Grandchildren run, my blood grows cold,
I promise to watch from beyond the realm!

DISSIDENCE

Shocking arguments are made
And friendships really shatter,
Attempts are made at "change of heart,"
But, so far, nothing matters.

Absent from this interval
Agreements will not be advanced,
Opinions gather true momentum,
Never sectile at a glance.

Raging speeches tend to cut into
The mind of innocents,
Causing tension, emotions spent,
Sewing seeds of malcontent!

ECSTASY DENIED

College day, long gone by,
Lazy years ensue,
We passed glances between us,
No time to really pursue
Long nights and lazy days,
No time for only each other,
Not even for another,
Papers to write, courses to finish. . .

Years of climbing,
Careers in flux,
Decisions not fully helpful,
Transcontinental rovings meant
To boost positions, but doubtful.

Considerations hanging,
Troublesome in their presence,

You were not among my ultimate choices
But neither I in yours!

HALLUCINATION

Is a phantasm present,
I thought I was alone,
Yet when I looked, a shadow
seemingly passed, resembling a clone.

A familiar visage floated
Before my very eyes,
The image flitted back and forth
Vainglorious like you and wise.

I'm alone, I know it,
Perspectives can be altered,
Misapprehension deceives me,
Believe me, I faltered.

Illusory patterns make their mark,
Reminiscent of days past,
Transporting minds easily impacted,
Delirium enters fast!

BLACK PEARLS

Searching in the water,
Years on end,
Not much came to the fore,
Much time to defend!

Did you check the appropriate beds?
Jewelers threads do justice,
Spinning, swinging, knotting, stretching,
Expecting something lustrous!

This morning is so bright and clear,
The boats are stocked with gear,
We gently pass into the cay,
Blue skies top the day!

We anticipate our luck,
The oyster beds are near,
Perhaps we'll find more treasure there
Than previous trips. No fear!

Said from our men in hip-high boots,
Their faces energized,
Their fingers holding gems so black,
"They're green—What a prize!"

GREEN TIES

We needed food to feed the hogs
And there, matching my daisy,
One bag stood out amongst the rest
Leaning against the wood-burning stove!

My hopes ran high that the yellow one
Would be the one he'd choose,
And often if you think real hard,
Your wishes will come true!

There were so many hogs,
They ate so much and soon,
The bag was empty,
How beautiful I would look in that,
Made into a dress!

I never could have imagined,
The picture I'd present,
A yellow dress, all clean and starched
Made smooth by lots of work!

More creative, she couldn't have been,
Mom's talent, so impressive,
Precisely sewn, exquisitely trimmed,
Green organdy, banded in yellow!

SUCCESSION

Parades in progress, coaches appear, and
Black-plumed horses dance,
They raise their heads and velvet blankets
Toggle as they prance!

The queen appears, the king is dead,
The servants gather 'round,
Coronation appurtenances all arranged,
How deftly they confound!

The scepter raised, the ring is donned,
Quiet falls like dew,
Amidst the crowds colors blush
In very muted hues.

Born to this occasion,
He stands with glittering crown,

His subjects and the common court
 Are gently kneeling down!

TWO RAINBOWS

My friend and I ran to the well,
Peeping quickly in,
It seemed so deep and damp and dark
We clanged the bell above!

Then we scurried to the trees,
Standing erect and swaying,
We rested underneath,
Tired from our running!

A cloudy day? That did not do
Our day any harm,
We survived the rainstorm and
Easily paddled in puddles.

With a few rays of sunlight
Shining through the trees,
We moved beyond the hanging limbs
And focused on a sight!

Multicolored arcs before us,
Took my friend's attention,
But always looking for other things,
I saw the rainbow behind us!

RESTORATION

Much is in upheaval,
Night comes super quick,
We run, we roam, and then return
To rebuild brick by brick!

Our emotions bubble over,
Our tangible mem'ries lost,
We look, we sit, we stand, we cry,
As if by nature tossed.

Distant in my memory,
A scene remains transfixed,
It comes and goes and comes again,
Feelings profoundly mixed.

Consistently surrounded by new ideas to make
A replication of something old, yet wanted once again,

I listen and I labor and never am I idle,
The sweat upon my brow reveals freedom from the pain.

CRYSTAL VASES

Roses in their beauty
Are held for all to see,
By glass with bubbles placed
Upon the sides—intricately!

As centerpiece or sideshow,
Their gleams catch all the eyes,
The sparkles, prisms, rainbow glints,
Engender concomitant sighs!

Careful if you remove them,
They require your rapt attention,
And necessary polishing follows
All their presentations!

FASCINATION

Mirrored lakes and snowy peaks,
Take our breath away,
Some vast expanses of ocean
Decline into a bay!

Magnolias, dogwoods, cherry trees,
Thrust their scents abroad,
Restructuring our senses,
Some on overload.

Pull petals from peonies,
Tiptoe through the clover,
Delight is found in these pursuits,
How pleasing to the lovers!

PUERILE ATTITUDES

We conversed and others listened
As we made our points so clear,
We laid the facts out, one by one,
And disagreed on some.

Unable to agree,
We definitely stood our ground
Respecting superiors is common
But what one knows, one knows!

See what is presented
And if your defense is faulty,
Swallow your pride, consider the facts,
Admit the clear path shown!

Difficulties often arise,
When faces must be saved,
It is possible to admit
My plan has merit too?

Perhaps you can,

Perhaps you can't

We'll see what finally comes. . .

RESENTMENT

Standing alone, late at night
I watched as breezes swirled,
The tables arranged,
The chairs free-standing,
Cloths draping; softly curled.

So many times I've come,
The party is always grand,
The grounds, the streamers,
How gorgeous you look
Is more than I can stand.

Perfection doesn't come often,
In fact it eludes my grasp;

My wish is only for parity,
Which can be secured
As in a pinkie clasp!

SYLVAN LEANINGS

We all have predilections
For our favored environs,
And sometimes jobs and circumstances
Impinge upon our choices.

We take the train, the car, the bus,
Arrive in urban centers,
Dodge the street vents, crash the sidewalks,
Walk the malls with ease!

Weekdays in this setting,
Wear upon the mind,
Glass and tile and brass and concrete,
Needs arise for choices!

Trees and knee-high grass,
Dirt roads and mud puddles,
Vegetable gardens, animal holdings,
Flowers circling trees!

Weeping willows bending low,
Oaks with no falling leaves,
Pine trees, blackberries, dewberries, all
Ornamental grasses, too!

SOPHISTICATION

Concern for the edges of a crystal vase,
The pearls around a frame,
Sounds received in this my space
Of elemental jazz.

Can elegant enshrouding
Calm the jittery soul,
Wrapping, encircling, swaddling chiffon,
Brings luxuries untold!

Attitude aloof!
Silent stars reveal,
The ever-changing swings and mood
And atmosphere surreal.

Glide within the prescribed arcs,
Sit with majesty!

Rise again! O aloof one
Devoid of tragedy!

LIKE SEMELE

We watched the tide ebb and flow,
Then walked for many days,
To find shelter, if we could,
Await our rescue team!

We ate the pickings 'round us,
We hovered in the caves,
We slept in shifts awakening
Finally to sea breezes!

Isolation left us with
No others to consider,
We landed here by accident,
We had not known each other prior!

As is the way of opposites,
Who tend to attract each other,
We stared, we glared, we talked,
We ate, we laughed considering survival!

Feeling safe, and yet deprived
Our time was further extended,
No one was coming for us,
We lapsed into reality!

Our interest in each other grew;
Our options had dwindled,
We laughed we kissed and then we cried,
Nature overtaking!

Many of life's experiences
Passed my recollection,
But never did I remember
Being overrun by passion!

LUMINOSITY

Your thoughts alone
Are given to a knowing kind of rest
Upon the pillars of my mind this day!

Tomorrow I shall reason
that they're only temporary,
Lending prominence of an illuminative day.

Points of sheer lucidity,
Conform to mounds of transluscence,
Defining special shades of pink and yellow
Rising to latent gleaming!

PATRIE/HEIMAT
(Native land)

Cold chills run my spine,
My speech is stymied,
My thoughts of you invade my mind,
Ideals consume my time!

Looking upward, I watch your flag,
Units marching by,
Children behind us playing tag,
Their spirits never sag!

Emotions run so deeply
On patriotic occasions,
Regiments climbing steeply,
The aged following feebly!

What I felt as a child must be truly real,
My loyalty unquestioned,

I stand at attention on even keel,
 The music stokes my zeal!

EMINENT RESTRAINT

Word had come of the betrayal,
Yet silently I pondered
All the days and nights gone by
and then I wondered,
If I could remain and wear outwardly,
The mask of sheer chicanery!
Stand tall, walk bold, and then
Display the ultimate in trickery!

Protecting my covey was my goal,
Perhaps diaphanous in my actions,
Yet in a way quite admirable
My gossamer act gained traction!

TRUST

Will the water that you bring,
Be free and clear of hate,
The foods you gather in this hour,
Be without debate?

The little hand that reaches out
Communicates a need,
To see and feel and touch your face
Without a word or deed!

When your eyes mirror kindness
When your face offers love,
The factors left for all to see,
Delivered from above!

INDOMITABLE SPIRIT

(For Mary Bell Krausz)

For years I watched your work
And was often reminded of gatherings,
That happened at the feet of our elite,
We, by their intellect, blinded!

You taught them long,
You taught them well,
They blossomed in your presence,
Respectful of your comprehensive breadth of knowledge,
Exhibiting excellence!
They'll long remember what you brought
To bear on their existence,

They'll stall and foment, then they'll rise,
remembering your persistence.

Gains are measured not
As inches, as feet, as lengths,
But in the constant drive towards
Information, wisdom, and strength!

You absolutely gave it all,
Even when you had nothing left to give,
We applaud your passage and what you left is
here!
It forever lives!

RECIPROSITY

Give me all your love,
Give me all your treasures,
Grant me access to your friends,
What shall I offer, pleasure?

If you refuse, I don't know
What to offer, yet again,
If you accept you give me cause
To turn my face from pain!

It would be good to match your thoughts
And lend my token kiss,
To all that is refined and pointing
To our pending bliss!

BLACK LACE

The drinks were brought before us,
The rusty pretzels dangle,
Tonight we were exquisitely attired,
Long silk threads and spangles!

Tablecloths in toasty ecru,
Flowers floating in water,
Candle holders lending light,
Loose sparkles; no bother!

The band was playing soothingly,
Strings kissing the atmosphere,
Black and white piano keys,
Spreading music, without peer!

Without a perfect spotlight or
Other prominent disclosure,
They entered, sat, and ordered something fruity,
Perhaps ambrosia!

The splits of champagne followed,
They chatted, giggled, and pranced,
The rustle of their dresses,
Caught our attention, as they danced!

Through glints of light
When they returned,
We watched their coming in awe,
Very sure of what we'd see: So attractive!
We dropped our jaws!

As each of their dress folds fell,
Red and green satin covered by lace,
We adjusted our ties and realized,
How elegant their taste!

RESPLENDENCE

Expectations raised, gently lending ways,
To praise appearances seen
And antiquities cleaned to perfection
by substances untold,
Yet from secret sources gleaned.

With habitual neck jerks,
Eyes and ears lurk
To find splendor hidden from view
yet tenderly spread in
Defining ways to titillate the resonance
And intensify the vibrations of beauty.

Eclat!

PARISIAN GARDEN

Circles, squares, rectangles,
All present in the plan,
Purples, oranges, whites and pinks,
Blooming without a ban!

When we come in our eyes are drawn
To colors dear to us,
We follow the paths, sit quietly down,
Admiring as we must!

Statues in the distance,
Hills clearly in view,
Greenery on every side,
Difficult to bid adieu!

A bench beside the water
Gives a brief reprieve,
Peach-tinged roses and
stark white petunias,
Fragrances to breathe!

Hours on end I'll sit and watch
The water chickens swim,
Bathed in history, drenched in shadows,
Evening sunlight dims!

INSPIRATION UNLIMITED

We arrived and all we saw
Were seas of people! Beautiful!
Diverse, tall, intelligent, short!
Contradictory? Dutiful?

Speeches were made, lectures given
And we began our journey,
Through the corridors of education,
Running straight ahead; no turning!

Stage plays and musical shows,
Sports events without measure.
A furor of classes, long campus walks,
Libraries, a bounteous treasure!

Hollywood stars, performing artists,
Poets and world-famous speakers,
Enter our presence, scattering elements
Amongst intellectual seekers.

PREJUDICE

Mindless anomalies!
Bantering comments!
Hurtful dispositions!
Obstructed vision!

Through the ages men have brought
Their teachings to the fore,
They ruminate and contaminate
Posterity all the more.

Angry visages and angrier words,
Poison to the souls,
That lurch and quiver, tremble, teeter,
Stretched to opposite poles!

The natural state exemplifies good,
The opposite engenders hate,
And in the scheme of exposure,
Perchance: Hades gate?

Born without a worry,
Born without a care,
The legacy they will incur
Conspicuous in their forebears!

INCANDESCENT CHARM

Walking on the avenue,
Hair flowing, breezes blowing,
To gently lift the curls off her shoulders,
Never, her pace, slowing!

She is followed and watched and ogled,
She never loses a step,
She stops, she chats, and then she smiles!
"Did she turn right?" "No left!"

We continued to observe from across the street:
A smile that rivaled neon!
Stares were angled from vantage points,
Her promenade was done!

LENA SMITH CARTER

Lena Smith Carter is an internationally renowned concert artist who has sung the poetry of the world in seven languages across America and around the world. She is a graduate of Central State University (OH) with a B. S. in Music Education, a graduate of Miami University (OH) with an M.Mus. in Performance and Repertory, and has studied for her doctorate at the Paris American Academy, Paris, France and The Pennsylvania State University, University Park, PA. Her international travels have taken her from Paris to New York as well as Porto Alegre, RS; Fortaleza, CE; Recife, PE; Joao Pessoa, PB: Natal, RN; Sergipe, AR; and Brasilia, DF, where she appeared at Casa Thomas Jefferson /The American Embassy. Her experiences in the Northeast allowed her to use many Brazilian folk songs as both the land and the language are very close to the hearts of northeasterners. In the south of Brazil, where there are many foreign-born citizens who speak other languages natively, she used more German, Latin, Italian, French, and Spanish, as well as Portuguese and English.

In addition to her concert career and international travels, she is a teacher, published poet and author; parent, publisher, patent holder, and philosopher. She has traveled to more than 15 different countries and has had more than thirty-five years experience in the creative arts and education. Her poetry is bold, original, colorful, and imaginative.

You may contact her directly at:

dseyafanel@hotmail.com.

Your positive comments are welcome and she will respond with information about forthcoming publications and workshop availability.

www.ingramcontent.com/pod-product-compliance
Lightning Source LLC
Chambersburg PA
CBHW032303150426
43195CB00008BA/561